March 11, 2019

To Daris —

much love and joy,

Janice P. Clark

Our InVisible World

Reflections on the awesome loving power of God within each of us

Bill Anderson and Annie P. Clark

BALBOA PRESS
A DIVISION OF HAY HOUSE

Copyright © 2018 Bill Anderson and Annie P. Clark.

All rights reserved. No part of this book may be used or reproduced by any means, graphic, electronic, or mechanical, including photocopying, recording, taping or by any information storage retrieval system without the written permission of the authors except in the case of brief quotations embodied in critical articles and reviews.

Balboa Press books may be ordered through booksellers or by contacting:

Balboa Press
A Division of Hay House
1663 Liberty Drive
Bloomington, IN 47403
www.balboapress.com
1 (877) 407-4847

Because of the dynamic nature of the Internet, any web addresses or links contained in this book may have changed since publication and may no longer be valid. The views expressed in this work are solely those of the authors and do not necessarily reflect the views of the publisher, and the publisher hereby disclaims any responsibility for them.

The authors of this book do not dispense medical advice or prescribe the use of any technique as a form of treatment for physical, emotional, or medical problems without the advice of a physician, either directly or indirectly. The intent of the authors is only to offer information of a general nature to help you in your quest for emotional and spiritual well-being. In the event you use any of the information in this book for yourself, which is your constitutional right, the authors and the publisher assume no responsibility for your actions.

Any people depicted in stock imagery provided by Getty Images are models, and such images are being used for illustrative purposes only. Certain stock imagery © Getty Images.

Print information available on the last page.

ISBN: 978-1-9822-1040-3 (sc)
ISBN: 978-1-9822-1038-0 (hc)
ISBN: 978-1-9822-1039-7 (e)

Library of Congress Control Number: 2018909651

Balboa Press rev. date: 08/29/2018

Contents

Foreword ix
Introduction xi
Acknowledgements xiii

1	The Power of Knowing	1
2	The Power of Belief	7
3	The Power of Courage	13
4	The Power of Forgiving	19
5	The Power of Hope	27
6	The Power of Joy	33
7	The Power of Giving	39
8	The Power of Love	47
9	The Power of Peace	55
10	The Power of Gratitude	61
11	The Power of Prayer	69
12	The Power of Stillness	79

Epilogue 87

*This book is dedicated to all who desire a deeper
and more personal relationship with the
Infinite InVisible Presence.*

Foreword

The dialogue between Annie and Bill can be likened to a couple of old friends having a fireside chat on a rainy afternoon while sipping a cup of hot tea. The conversation becomes their personal testimonies of how certain passages from the Holy Bible have influenced their lives. You, the reader, are privy to their journey as you eavesdrop on their wisdom.

The authenticity of the dialogue is far-reaching. You may very well find yourself becoming an invisible participant in their conversation as you reflect on new and profound ways to interpret the spiritual inferences contained in the passages as well as consider how you may apply them to your life in a practical way. You, the reader, may very well be catapulted into contemplative meditation after each discussion.

The writers give examples of how they have deliberately or unconsciously experienced the universal principles contained in their selected scriptures by reflecting on the inner meaning. They recall their "wins" when they were in alignment with the concepts as well as their "challenges" when they were not in alignment. The Truth Principles discussed here ignite a feeling of unlimited possibilities. Each discourse ushers the reader into a deeper inquiry into his or her own spiritual convictions.

The title, *Our InVisible World*, suggests there exists—within each one of us—unseen forces that are made up of feelings, emotions, thoughts, beliefs, memories and fears that influence our visible world moment by moment. It further implies that a negative force may be transformed at any time by the renewing of one's mind.

The writers reinforce the good news: there are inherent feelings/forces of *Love, Joy, Peace, Harmony, Beauty and Wisdom* that are unchanging in their nature. These forces are the very essence of *Our InVisible World*. They are the "…lo, I AM with thee always" (Matthew 28:20 KJV).

Annie and Bill teach us that certain mental attitudes and physical practices support us in unleashing our natural goodness—thereby letting it be on Earth as it is in *Our InVisible World*. This inspiring message is one that the reader may turn to time and time again for support, encouragement, and sheer joy.

> *Congratulations Annie and Bill for bringing forth this creative work and filling the following pages with your insights!*

Reverend Mary Louise Ruffner
Founder, Co-director
StillPoint Spiritual Center

Introduction

When we met just over two years ago we seemed to be on similar quests—to continuously examine, explore, and uncover (or discover) our understanding of our inner knowing, desires, and reliance on that which is InVisible. Our first several meetings were two-hour sessions of prayer, meditation, and agreeing upon what we each received from our personal time while being still in the silence.

Silence! Stillness! Those two revelations were major as we embarked upon our quest for bringing to our awareness what our personal spiritual journeys revealed. We continued in prayer, meditation, journaling, and sharing—always seeking to know more of what God, revealed to us through *our inner InVisible worlds.*

Now we aspire to share our experiences with you, dear readers, and perhaps in some small way inspire you to continue (or begin) your own search for spiritual enlightenment.

Your experiences may be the same or similar to ours or they may be very different—but always valid. We each approach our Creator in our own ways and all ways by whatever means we consciously and reverently connect to that which we name or not name to glorifying that which is our Source. At the same time, we are aware that we cannot ever confine that which cannot be confined.

We call the Creative Intelligence God, or the Infinite Indwelling Presence, or LORD or some other name or expression. All names or words that resonates with you are just as valid as those with which we identify.

Our sincerest desire is that this small book will be of value to you as you continue your spiritual journey.

Annie P. Clark and Bill Anderson

Acknowledgements

There are so many persons who offered both encouragement and editing skills while this book was in process. Here we name but a few: The Reverend Mary Louise Ruffner, Practitioner Emeritus Ann Gay, Jean Anderson, Amy Chamberlain, Carrie Chamberlain, Randy Rock, and Alsandyra Essien.

An especial thanks to our families whose love, encouragement, and faith in us never wavered.

We also thank our publisher Balboa for their expert assistance.

But mostly, we are deeply grateful for that *InVisible Presence* that kept moving us forward even when we seemed to be at a standstill.

1
The Power of Knowing

> "...Know the truth and the truth shall set you free."
>
> John 8:32 NIV

Annie:

Knowing, for me, is proving by application or activity that which I believe. Knowing is also having complete confidence in the *InVisible* without validation from others. I am often reminded of the powerful statement in John 8:32. I understand this to mean that I will be free to make the right decision because now I have the tool, the courage, and the confidence to deal with whatever issue or concern I have now.

Knowing, then, is experiencing. Our words often fall on deaf ears when we try to console another who is grief stricken by the death of a child or a parent by saying: "I know what you are going through" when, in fact, we have not yet experienced what they are experiencing. We can only imagine how we would feel, especially if we are childless.

Something deep within us knows everything; however, in our conscious state we do not know that we know until and unless we ask the Infinite Indwelling Presence that which we desire to know.

Years ago, I needed to do a certain job on the computer at a time when there were very few software programs that could accomplish what was to be done. However, I knew that what I wanted to do was possible (for with God, nothing is impossible). I had programming knowledge, but not for the specific task. I consulted with learned colleagues who also did not know how to accomplish the task.

Yet, at the very core of my being I knew that the activity was possible and that I could do it. So confident was I that I went to bed with the conscious awareness that upon awakening I would know exactly what to do. I don't remember dreaming of the solution—all I know is that when I awoke the next morning I knew exactly how to write the program. It took six hours of dedicated pursuit, which when finished, worked perfectly the first time.

I am reminded of Thomas Alva Edison, who knew that he could produce an incandescent light bulb and, though he experimented time after time without success, remained persistent. Something within him, *"the knower"* urged him on until he succeeded.

Bill:

The divine Spirit that is part of each of us knows all. This knowing is not based on any doubt. It is absolute, pure truth. Each day when you awaken it is a reminder that you can know God is always with you.

The difference between a belief and knowing is not having any doubt. Some may believe Jesus loves them, yet they have doubt at times if this is possible. The person who goes within and can connect to the Universal Source, the energy of God that each of us have, experiences the bliss of knowing they are a part of God.

Knowing is a wonderful gift I am grateful for knowing. I take time each day to go within and just relax for a few moments to calm my physical body and recharge my spiritual side.

Many times, at work you might hear someone try to gossip about a co-worker. They will start by saying: "Did you know…?" about someone. My response is always simple: "I do not know that." This simple response generally stops the conversation and prevents my energy from being pulled into gossip. In this example the other person may believe something to be true about someone, but their ego wants to gather others on their side.

A good teacher of mine used to challenge me when I would say that I know I am part of God. She would ask do you truly feel you are part of God? Or do you just believe it? If you only believe you are part of the Holy Spirit you will still have doubts. Once you cross over in consciousness to *knowing* you are, then you will see God's love in everything without any doubt.

Knowing is an energy that is a perfect, whole, and complete place within everyone. Knowing allows you to connect to the one Mind of God. If each person took 10% of the time daily that they dedicate to busyness, e.g., watching T.V., and spent this time in quiet meditation, the whole consciousness of mankind would be raised to a higher positive level of Peace, Love, and Joy.

To eliminate doubt, make a choice to connect with God within you. By quieting the mind and going within even for just a few moments, you will understand the feeling for yourself of being connected in Spirit to your divine self. This is a personal journey. It is unnecessary to convince others, but just simply observe how you have changed and what you attract into your life knowing you are one with the Holy Spirit. It's amazing how quickly your life will change.

I choose not to announce I am a spiritual being. I know I am, and the energy I focus on from Source can do anything. I live my life by example so if others ask, "Why are you calm, stress-free, and at peace with all the chaos going on at work or home?", I can then tell them my story and know that when they are ready, they will seek their own spiritual path.

I am energy

I am Light

I am one with God

I know that God is everything and everywhere.

2

The Power of Belief

> *"And without faith it is impossible to please God, because anyone who comes to him must believe that he exists …."*
>
> Hebrews 11:6 NIV

Annie:

Belief comes from an awareness deep within me that resonates with what is truth. It is extremely hard to explain how and why I immediately believe or not believe. Something within me urges me to accept or deny.

Perhaps the *Power of Belief* is the same as the *power of intuition* when I hear that small, quiet voice (or nudging) within to act now. There have been many instances when I felt strongly to move in a direction without any visible proof that it would be the correct thing to do – however, it always turned out to be so.

Long before cell phones were popular, I relocated to southern California. While driving late at night I exited the freeway at the wrong place and ended up in a dark parking area of a warehouse complex. However, I had a sincere belief that I was guided and protected. This included a belief that I would not experience any vehicular problems. I absolutely knew that I was safe and would continue to be so.

I maneuvered my back to the freeway, accessed the proper direction, and continued to the exit that led me home.

Another instance of this awesome *Power of Belief* was when I was informed that I needed major surgery. I was unafraid. I sincerely believed that the surgery would be successful. However, several weeks prior to the scheduled surgery, I experienced what I thought was a heart condition. My internist examined me thoroughly, including an electric cardiogram, which proved that my heart was healthy. What I experienced was an extreme episode of acid reflex. My physician prescribed several remedies which cleared up the symptoms. Again, I believed that all was well.

I went forth with the surgery with a strong belief that all was well, and that I need not worry about the outcome because I was always in the heart and care of God. And, of course, surgery and recuperation went as planned.

The *Power of Belief* is that which allows me to accomplish that which I am to do — all the time.

I often ask myself again and again, "Just what is this belief that is at the very core and essence of my being?" The response is always the same: "There is a power and a presence that is present everywhere which created me; which provides for me and sustains me; which guides me and gently reminds me when to take a different path, and which always accepts me just as I am."

I believe in the goodness of my fellow beings, that all are desirous of the same things I yearn for — joy, peace, love, and a sense of well-being. I believe that we are born into families so that we will know that we "belong" as well as having others to care for and about.

Bill:

We all have different belief systems that we operate by. Our beliefs are learned from our individual life lessons. Some of these beliefs are in place to protect us. Others are the beliefs passed to us from our surroundings, our parents, our teachers, our friends, or even the television shows we watched growing up.

I was raised in an interfaith home. My mother was Pentecostal. From the age of two, my Jewish stepfather helped raise me. My mother believed in Jesus Christ and made sure I attended Sunday School every week. My stepfather, being Jewish, demonstrated how he lived based on his faiths and beliefs.

It was a huge lesson in life watching and observing, over the years, the tolerance showed by my mom's family when discussing religion with my step-father. Both sides agreed to allow the other to have their beliefs without trying to force someone to convert to their belief system and religion.

> *I am aligned with Spirit*
> *I am an observer in the physical world.*

Belief is something that is learned and can be changed. We must allow ourselves to grow in knowledge based on the spiritual paths each of us are on as individual expressions of the divine. The right teachers or lessons will be given to us as we need them on this lifetime journey.

As a child, I was taught to believe that God will handle everything. As I grew and asked questions, I also learned that God, Holy Spirit, the I AM within each of us is the power we use to create our own worlds. Our thoughts and the words we choose have power in them.

Evolution of the soul is to understand your true relationship to God. There are stages we all go through as we learn and build our belief system. Since beliefs are influenced by our environment, we need to take time to reflect: "Does this particular belief still serve the highest good of all concerned? Is it time to let go of one belief to make room for new beliefs that will enable us to move farther along our spiritual paths?"

Ask yourself what beliefs still serve you and which ones you need to change.

> *I am connected to Holy Spirit.*

3

The Power of Courage

"Be strong and courageous. Do not be afraid or terrified because of them, for the LORD your God goes with you; he will never leave you nor forsake you."

Deuteronomy 31:6 NIV

"Have I not commanded you? Be strong and courageous. Do not be afraid; do not be discouraged, for the LORD your God will be with you wherever you go."

Joshua 1:9 NIV

Annie:

Whenever I face an issue that seems to overwhelm me, I am reminded that the Infinite Loving Presence of God is right where I am. The Old Testament passages cited at the start of this chapter remind me that I have the strength needed to move through any situation.

The *Power of Courage* will take us through all the places that we fear.

A colleague of mine who was recuperating from a serious illness wanted to perform tasks that would jeopardize her recovery. She was feeling good, became restless, and did not want to stay in bed. However, a very wise person informed her that it took courage *to do nothing*.

The *Power of Courage* allows us to not only speak out when we witness injustices but also to work towards a solution for the highest and best good of all involved. That well-spring of courage at the very core of our being continuously provides the stamina needed to be fearless when confronted with a seemingly dangerous situation.

Courage and faith go hand in hand. Remember: God is always, and in all ways, supplying what is needed, when needed. God supplies the courage to do what we are called to do. All we need do is to stop our fear-filled thoughts and remember again that with God, all that all that is needed to accomplish the task at hand is possible, NOW!

There is no fear in love; but perfect love casts out fear.

Bill:

The *Power of Courage* is to face the unknown and have no fear. When you come from a place of Spirit within you of love, peace, and joy, you can do anything. You are presented with opportunities to show your courage in many ways.

As an example, you may be asked to speak in front of a group of people. By first calming yourself and knowing you are planting seeds that will help others, you can speak to any size group.

When you speak to a small group, you gain confidence to speak to a larger group. Very few great public speakers started by talking in front of an audience with 1,000 people. They practiced as they connected to the courage each of us has within to succeed.

Letting go of self-judgement allows you to realize you are an instrument of God passing on information that will help others. When you connect to the service energy of the Holy Spirit, you can and will amaze yourself and inspire your audience. Courage is also the ability to listen to others to understand what is being said—not interrupting or listening to just provide an answer. When you are an active listener, you learn more. When you are a speaker, you can show courage by calling out others and by challenging them to listen.

Courage starts by believing in yourself and knowing the soul level we are all love. We are all created in the image and likeness of God. When you radiate the inner splendor of Love, everyone you come into contact will and feel your energy calming them.

As a child you are given the opportunity to stand up and help a friend who may need your assistance. As an adult you have new lessons and will still be presented opportunities to show courage by doing what is right for your family and friends. Most of all, you can demonstrate courage by doing what is right for you.

I am strong and powerful
I am bold
I am a good listener
I am Love, Loving, and Lovable
I am peace
I am Joy
I am Inner Splendor
I am endless possibilities
I am connected to all
I am inspired to do what is right
I am vocal
I am sharing my thoughts to help others
I am more than just my physical Me

I start each day by being grateful, allowing my mind, body, and spirit to be consciously connected with Divine guidance, = knowing I have the courage to accomplish anything. As a result, nothing can stand in my way except my own fears. So, I remind myself that I have my own self-approval, and that I am divinely guided to shine my light and to help others.

4

The Power of Forgiving

"Then Peter came and said to Him, "Lord, many times shall I forgive my brother or sister who sins against me? Up to seven times?" Jesus answered, "I tell you not seven times, but seventy times seven.
Matthew 18:21-22 NIV

"Forgive us our sins, for we also forgive everyone who sins against us…"
Luke 11:4 NIV

Annie:

How many times are we to forgive one that trespasses against us? According to Matthew 18:21-22, seventy times seven. Wow! Four hundred and ninety times—or, as many times as necessary. In my lifetime there is someone that I have forgiven at least these many times. "Who?" you might ask. *Me!* Why me? Because I continuously trespass or do that which I ought not.

My most recent revelation on the *Power of Forgiveness* came when I was practicing what I would say to a dear woman who had entrusted me with a prized possession that I inadvertently mutilated. It became very clear that I was planning to ask her to forgive me even though I had not forgiven myself.

The more I prayed for forgiveness from her and from God, the more I felt troubled. I confessed my wrong doing with my daughter and then with several others but had not yet the courage to approach the one whom I had let down. She was unaware of what I had done.

Then, as I prayed, I was gifted by the grace of God to first forgive myself—that looming plank in my own awareness—before approaching another to ask forgiveness.

The words in the Lord's Prayer: "Forgive us our trespasses" had not been accepted by me. And then I realized that I was expecting another to forgive me when I was unwilling to do the same. I then began to forgive myself and soon felt worthy enough to ask another to do the same. Needless to say, when I confessed to the person involved, she immediately forgave me.

Out of ignorance there have been many times when I felt guilty of doing something for which I did not have the power to do. For years I carried around a guilt thinking that I had the power over another's life which only God had. When I realized this, I was able to forgive myself for thinking that I was in charge of anyone other than myself.

Bill:

Being able to forgive and let go of the past is a very freeing feeling. By forgiving others, you allow yourself to move forward without carrying any negative feelings.

Many of us hold on to blame and shame for decisions we made when we were younger. One of the first things you can do to improve your life is to forgive yourself. If you had a failed relationship, a family member you argued with, or a job from which you were fired, remember that the past is the past. You must live fully in the present moment to move forward on your spiritual path.

Take time each day to tell yourself: *I am better than I used to be. I accept myself. I approve of myself. I let go of the past and move forward.*

As an employer, I had to let people go who did not do their jobs well. When my business lost income from clients, I also had the unfortunate task of letting good workers go. For years I had carried the idea that I had failed as a leader in protecting my employees from being laid off. Over the years I have met several of former employees who told me that working for me was the happiest, most rewarding job they had ever had. Most had used the experience to move forward into larger companies and were earning more than my small business would have been able could pay.

Remember that God has a plan and that that plan may not be what you see at the time (See Jeremiah 29:11). However, if you work from a place of love and light, you will always do what is best for yourself and for others. The result for me was limiting myself by not wanting a job that I would have lay people off.

However, the universe had other plans for me and as a manager within several Fortune 100 companies I found myself faced with the same situation of having to hire and fire people. I tried to make the transition period as easy as I could for the person in question, explaining why this change was happening and assisting them as they found new work in other companies. During this time, I found my skills of coaching and mentoring others came from the lessons I had learned from my past mistakes.

Eventually, I found myself laid off from a large Fortune 100 company. I knew I had to quickly forgive the company, my boss, my co-workers, and myself. And I did. Within two weeks, I found a new job and was inspired to help my new employer get its work done.

Looking back on my career, I have had many opportunities to express *forgiveness* to others.

Be in Spirit in all things you do, and positive outcomes will come your way. Avoid focusing on gossip; stop yourself from becoming one who looks at life and their work as half full. Allow your cup to run over with full abundance.

If anger or revenge is your first response when you think someone has intentionally done you wrong, stop! Then, detach from the situation. Ask yourself if it is just your ego's interpretation of what happened. In most cases, when you examine what happened you will see no one truly intended to harm you. Once you can conquer your ego's attempt to pull you off your spiritual path, you can let go, forgive and return to being in Spirit – a person who loves all.

The ability to not blame yourself for anything is another key to forgiveness. I have seen people carry a heavy load of blame with them for an entire lifetime. In order to move forward, it is necessary to let go of the past. forward. You cannot change what happened. Acknowledge it, learn from it, and move forward by approving of who you are today.

As we age we also tend to cling to our past stories. God wants us to be, have, and experience the fullness of love we are destined to receive and give fully.

Recently I was offered a new role that would double my salary. However, after I said no, questions came to me regarding my choice. Was it self-doubt? Was it intuition that it was not the right fit? Was there something from my own past I had to forgive myself for? By taking the time to reflect about my past and then by truly allowing myself to be forgiven—to not blame myself, and then to see myself surrounded by Universal Truth—I was able to move forward.

I am forgiven - I am one with Spirit.

See the light in others, and treat them as if
that is all you see.
Dr. Wayne Dyer

5

The Power of Hope

"For I know the plans I have for you," declares the Lord, "plans to prosper you and not to harm you, plans to give you hope and a future."
Jeremiah 29:11 NIV

Annie:

Hope is expecting that which we desire to occur in the future. Hope gives us something to look forward to. Hope defines our innate beliefs in the myriad of possibilities and opportunities life holds for us.

Without hope or a belief in a better world we can become discouraged and disenchanted. However, Hope is so powerful that we often are told to "just have hope" when our circumstances seem bleak. Hope is enmeshed with faith. As Hebrews 11:1 tells us: "Faith is the substance of things hoped for…the evidence of things not seen."

Hope has kept people alive for days without food. Hope has kept people alive for days in extreme cold—all because they had a hope for a better day of food and warmth.

We hope for the best life our children can experience. Our hope for them is to know that there is a power and presence at the very core and essence of their being that sustains them. Hope is powerful because we expect that which we desire to be realized.

One is often cautioned to be careful about what is hoped for (or asked for through prayer) as it does tend to show up in one form or another.

> *The natural flights of the human mind are not from pleasure to pleasure, but from hope to hope.*
> *Samuel Johnson*

Bill:

I have had many experiences in this lifetime. Sometimes they were great achievements, and other times they appear to be major disappointments. The one thing that you must have is Hope that all will be better.

In the short-term, God uses challenges and hurdles to help each of us grow stronger and move forward on our own divine path. The Universe also provides help for us to complete what we started. If you look at a situation only with the logical, physical mind you may become depressed and overwhelmed. However, you have a gift within you that knows the Truth and is always providing Hope that your situation will get better.

Examples include losing your job, breaking up or getting a divorce, or having a close family member or friend transition into the next phase of life. In each of these life changing situations you can choose to observe the situation through the eyes of God and see clearly how Hope will help you get through the challenge.

When the feeling of Hope seems to be lost you can get it back by simply being still and asking your higher soul self to show you a sign or remind you how to feel Hopeful about the situation.

Hope is a feeling of knowing—without any doubt— that everything will work out for your highest good. Endless possibilities are your divine right as a child of God.

Use "I am" statements as a reminder to yourself that you are being Hopeful.

God is / I am

Stay focused on what you want, and you will always have the feeling of Hope. Be optimistic always. No one knows everything.

Hope is the ability to:

- *see an outcome greater than others can see*
- *aim higher in life to accomplish your goals*
- *overlook an individual's opinion of you*
- *choosing to see a positive outcome to a situation...*
- *live a full and rewarding life, no matter what obstacles you face*
- *be confident you will succeed*

An artist has hope before ever starting a painting, a sculpture, or a design that they will create something they will love, and others will be amazed to behold. Like an engineer, we must have hope that we can building something that will outlast our lifetime and best serve others.

Peace is liberty in tranquility.
Marcus Tullius Cicero

6

The Power of Joy

"...weeping may stay for the night, but rejoicing comes in the morning..."

Psalm 30:5 NIV

"This is the day which the L*ord* *hath made; we will rejoice and be glad in it."*

Psalm 118:24, KJV

Annie

One of my favorite passages in the Holy Bible is "This is the day which the Lord hath made; we will rejoice and be glad in it." For me to rejoice I must know what joy is. In Psalm 30:5 I am reminded that can be returned. To me this means that after I empty myself of the anguish of sorrow, I am again filled with joy.

Joy is not a thing that I can see or touch—rather, it is a sense or feeling deep within me. It is *InVisible* as is love, peace, and gratitude.

Joy is that pleasant feeling that washes over us when we uncover or discover the answer to a question we pondered. Joy is the result of seeing a nearly forgotten friend. Joy is the rush of pride and happiness at the graduation of a child.

Only the Infinite Loving presence of God through the Indwelling Christ can give us joy. Consequently, no one can take our joy from us.

The *Power of Joy* reveals itself through quiet meditation–when we sit in the silence of our own being, fully present with the Infinite. Receiving good news reveals the unbridled *Power of Joy*.

The *Power of Joy* reveals itself as we become aware of yet another gift of God. This could happen as we prepare meals for our families or partake in a meal so lovingly prepared by another. The joy is expressed from our very core. Joy is the experience at the sight of the budding trees in the spring and the array of beauty in the summer flowers.

I have experienced what is known as "unspeakable moments of joy" such as when my grandchildren were declared healthy at birth; when my daughter's health was restored; and when my son recovered after his appendix ruptured during surgery.

During moments of joy, there is no depression or despondency–not even for a moment. Joy has the power to brighten an otherwise dark and dismal day.

Memories of joyful experiences and encounters are more powerful that sorrow. How joyful it is to remember our loved ones who have moved in to the next expression of eternal life.

The *Power of Joy* moves us through those difficult times.

Bill

I am Joy.

Joy is why we are here. In everything we do we seek to be happy, joyful, and merry. You can choose to have the feeling of Joy at any time, place, or event in your life. It is how you look at the situation.

The *Power of Joy* is pure connection to Source energy—the Holy Spirit within each of us. I have heard it said: "Do not let someone else take your joy." This can only happen in the physical world if allow others to determine if we will be happy. In the Spiritual world, we are always joyful and rejoicing.

I am grateful for the feeling that the joy within me is always with me. By being still in the moment, I can return my thoughts to that of joy.

An excellent place to practice being joyful is in traffic. If someone cuts you off or drives too fast or drives too close behind you – you can choose to remain joyful in the moment. Or you can allow the events of others to impact you by feeling anger. The anger you feel is from loss of control. Do not let anyone take your Joy.

Joy is that which all seek, and yet we have it with us always. Joy is your natural state of being. Joy is who I am as I connect with the Source of every Joy. Joy is a jubilation of life that can be celebrated every day. We each have a foundation of Joy within. Let our Joy overflow in all directions.

Joy will raise us up and beyond any feelings of loss, grief, or despair. Joy is the gift we all can share with each other; and, through this sharing, we can raise our collective energy.

Joy is a fundamental feeling of being in peace and happiness at the same time.

As you observed a child, watch and see how their joy is expressed. A child simply lives in the moment, playing, learning, and letting joy be part of their lives as they share it with others.

Remember your joy is inside you always.

*The present moment is filled with joy and happiness,
if you are attentive, you will experience it.*

7
The Power of Giving

> *"Bring the whole tithe into the storehouse, that there may be food in my house. Test me in this," says the* Lord *Almighty, "and see if I will not throw open the floodgates of heaven and pour out so much blessing that there will not be room enough to store it."*
>
> *Malachi 3:10 NIV*

Annie:

You cannot out give God.

The *Power of Giving* reveals to us that there is an inexhaustible supply of everything — and as we give we create a space to receive even more than we give. As we give from a place of love, we receive such a tremendous joy that it is as if we are the recipients instead of the givers.

The *Power of Giving* sometimes makes us think that we are the giver rather than an avenue through which God's supply is circulated. As we understand that we are not the giver but an avenue through which God is giving, we feel the *InVisible Presence* moving through us—that we are chosen to be ambassadors of good.

The *Power of Giving,* especially when we give of ourselves though loving and joyful service to another, rejuvenates us and restores our souls.

What is it that I must give? As I ponder this, I become aware that I have something that the recipient does not appear to have or believe that they lack at that moment. Sometimes what I must give is just a kind word of encouragement to someone who is otherwise feeling low. Sometimes I have money or something else of value to give — such as an article of clothing and sometimes I have my business skills to give. And sometimes, what I must give is a smile or a silent prayer on their behalf.

The *Power of Giving* allows me to honor and credit others for their various accomplishments.

Because God is both Source and Supplier of all, I am already supplied with what I am to give. I give from the overflow of what God had already entrusted to me to circulate.

The *Power of Giving* includes being truthful and straightforward. It also includes asking for forgiveness for any trespasses or neglect on my part.

Bill:

I AM (God is) Giving. What a wonderful energy you release and receive when you give. Just relax and think about how you feel when you receive a gift from the heart of someone who cared enough to give to you. Just remembering the act of kindness can attract more of this same energy towards you.

There is a universal law that says: "That to which you give your attention will grow." To transform your life, you simply must pay attention to the words, actions, and feelings to which you give your attention. You can give your ideas, talents, and loving compassion to everything you do in life.

It is said: "What you give, so shall you receive." Many examples of this exist. A simple example is President Bill Clinton. He could walk through a crowd meeting and greet people, shaking hands. After the event, many would say how they felt they had connected with him even if they had only spoken for 30 seconds. The key thing he did was give his full attention to the one person, even if it was brief— saying hello to a reporter, for example. The other persons felt good inside knowing they had connected even though it was just for a moment in time.

Each of your ideas has energy ascending with it. I have a friend who is an entrepreneur and has started many businesses. When he was young and starting out he did not want to share—he was very adamant about not having any partners in his business. Because of not being willing to give, he had limited success. He would see others take his similar idea and build huge businesses. When the product or service was similar, the difference was the energy he put into his business of putting up walls and barriers.

Over time, he began to give other opportunities to share in his business. He realized he could grow a much larger company faster by partnering with others rather than being on his own. The key to his success is in giving. The energy of giving keeps all things in circulation.

The Power of Giving is a gift that returns to us in many ways. By being of service and helping others who need our time, ideas, advice, or funds, we will know that we are on our spiritual paths and all is well.

An intern that was in his final semester as a chiropractor went on a mission trip to the Dominican Republic. His only goal was to help others. He already planned to return to his home town and continue a practice that his deceased father started. During the week he was away, he worked on a woman each day and was able to see a huge improvement in her health. This event changed the path he was on. He returned to the Dominican Republic and started his own practice there helping those who could not afford to see a doctor.

As an observer, it has been a wonderful experience to see this intern become a doctor. It has been equally wonderful to feel that the energy of his deceased father was with him on his journey.

I am a giving person
I give freely of my time and myself to help others.
I share my knowledge to help others move forward in life
I am blessed with having more than enough when I give.
I have an endless supply from the divine Source to give.
I am happy to give and serve my fellow mankind
I am an instrument that allows the energy of
the Holy Spirit to express through me.

I am more by giving of myself to others.

Less is more, this simple statement represents how you live your life.

By not hoarding and holding on to every item that you have ever known or touched you embody an important life lesson. You reach a point in life when you understand how it feels to give away belongings that are no longer needed. Giving clothes away that will help a homeless person, giving furniture away that you pay to store helps — free up space and money to be used for your highest good.

The process of giving helps with the Law of Circulation— providing new energy to flow into stagnant spaces. Often what you have increases when you do not hold on too tightly to what you currently possess.

Recently, I experienced this by moving from a house I had lived in for 20 years. I was amazed at how much stuff I had. Looking back, the move would have been much easier had I taken the time prior to moving to sort items into two basic groups: give away or keep.

Take stock of what you own and ask yourself what you have truly used and what you have forgotten you had them. You will be safe letting them go of your unused items.

We make a living by what we get, but
we make a life by what we give.
Winston Churchill

8

The Power of Love

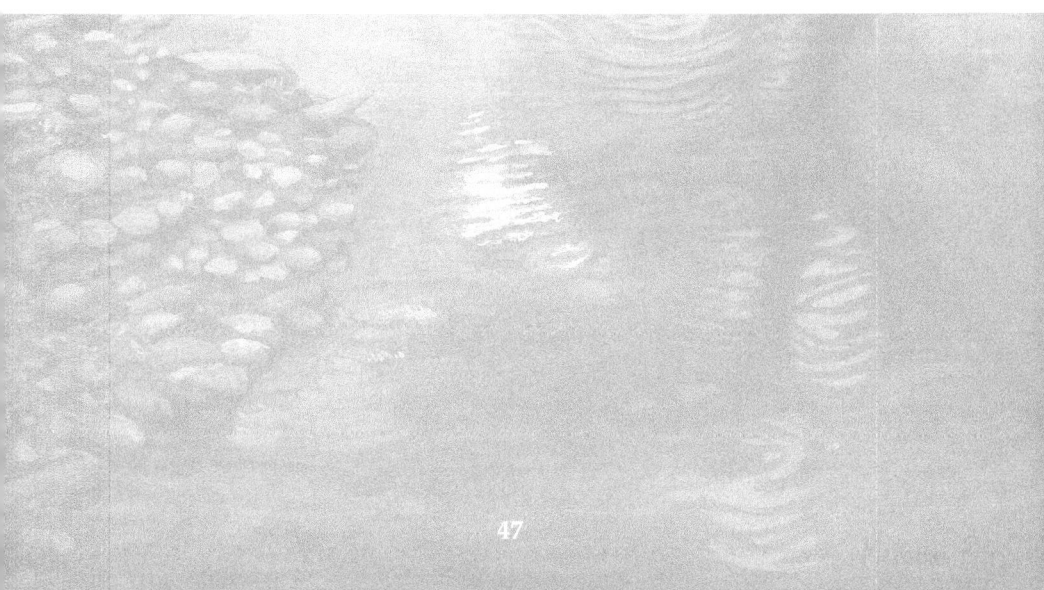

> *"...But the greatest of these is love"*
> *1 Cor 13:13 NIV*

> *"If you keep my commands, you will remain in my love, just as I have kept my Father's commands and remain in his love."*
> *John 15:10 NIV*

Annie:

Love is an *InVisible* powerful force that permeates all of existence. Love is at the core and essence of all that is.

Love is so powerful, yet it is so difficult to explain.

"I love you" is often stated as a parting greeting. A feeling of both belonging and being accepted "as is" comes to mind. As I ponder the awesome *Power of Love*— which is indeed *InVisible*—I recall that I have always had an innate knowing that I was and am loved. First by my parents and siblings, and then by neighbors, friends and colleagues, and especially from my spouse.

Over the years, however, I have pondered: "Just exactly what is love?" Periodically, many questions have arisen such as: "Where does love come from" or "What does love do? Is it conditional" and "What is its power? How many types of love are there?"

The first and foremost in my awareness is what is termed "unconditional," or the acceptance of life and people "as is". Love supports the emergence of life. A newborn babe seems to feel and sense this love.

My most amazing experiences of love occurred when I first beheld my children immediately after their births. Holding these small, beautiful expressions of love— love between my husband and I; miracles that came through me from the *Infinite Loving Presence* of God—opened a floodgate of appreciation and gratitude for life itself.

I was engulfed in the awareness of the unconditional love of God as I realized that I was entrusted with the care and nurturing of these two souls. This awareness brought on a new appreciation of my parents and how they managed a household of nine children through the same awesome *Power of Love*. As children, we know when we are loved. Love is that special bond between a parent and child, between husband wife, between siblings, and between others.

Because of God's love flowing from the very core and essence of my being, I was empowered to perform my motherly and parental duties with a sense of unspeakable joy.

Love is considerate of both others and self. "Love thy neighbor as thyself" is what we are instructed to do. Love is giving of self without measurement or requirement of a return. Yet, as we give there is always a receiving of something greater, a knowing within, of pure love.

The *Power of Love* has revealed itself to me many times— through quiet intuitive knowing—of what and how to do things of which I was not previously aware I could. My latest awareness of the awesome *Power of Love* revealed itself during a bout of illness. Cards and phone calls came daily. "I'm thinking of you" or "God is your health" or "just trust in the awesome power of God" were all reminders of how much we feel loved by others and by God.

The *Power of Love* continues to reveal to me that all is well in every circumstance regardless of my experiences. The *Power of Love* overwhelms and dissipates all discord. I am confident that I am loved "as is" through a sense of well-being.

The Power of Love has opened my heart to desire good for all people; in return, I feel this love reciprocating everywhere I go.

Love is complete, pure, kind, and compassionate. Love is comingled with joy– hence a deep and abiding satisfaction with life as it is.

Bill:

The *Power of Love* demonstrates to each of us that all things are perfect and whole. God is love. God is part of who we are. No matter what is going on in our lives, we can choose and remember we are part of this Infinite Love that surrounds us all at any time.

First, one must feel love for themselves. When you look in the mirror say: "I am loved. I love all things. I am desirable. I am Loving." Life must open to let my light shine in all directions.

Holy Spirit is everywhere and only knowing love. Love is an energy that always connects each of us to God. When meditating, one can focus on just seeing this word love on a blank canvas. Then allow yourself to fully feel the love of the universe that flows to you, through you, and surrounding you always. The feeling is that of total bliss.

For anyone with self-esteem issues, this is a wonderful way to start remembering you are already loved. Always.

By divine right, each person is loved, lovable, and has the ability to be loving to all – including themselves.

In state of love, you will know that everything is alright and will work out. You cannot love something and hate it at the same time.

You may know or see others that have forgotten that they are loved. Their actions may appear harmful to themselves and to others. You can send anyone love just by being still and sending the energy and *Power of Love*. Over time, you will be amazed how they change when they also know they are loved.

Affirmations you may want to repeat often to your self are:

*I am worth loving — the fact that I exist
means that I am worth loving.
I am lovable and worth loving.
I am Love
Love is within me
I am grateful for the greatest gift of all is Love
I am blessed with knowing I am Love, Loving and Lovable
Thank you! Thank you! Thank You!*

Practice:

Allow yourself to go within, to be present in the moment. Feel the energy of love that is part of your soul, part of the heart space. When you identify thoughts of the past, just let it go. Stay focused on being anew with yourself.

When you can sense and feel the time you experienced love within, then you can let your light shine brightly as you outwardly project your InVisible awareness of love.

I Am Love is a powerful statement to believe. It is about a spiritual love, a love with no end, a love you can choose to see all things through.

Being in spiritual love is a love for all things and knowing at the essence all things come from Love. A wonderful thing about being able to feel spiritual Love is that it is always present. You do not have to do anything but allow your mind to go to the space in your heart where you can feel love at any time. Just let go of anything that is not love and feel the self-acceptance of who and why you are here.

Reclaim your ability to love. Affirm:

Everything that God is I am.
You, I, and God are connected as one.
You and I are connected to all the love of God.
I AM pure spirit.
My life is an expression of spiritual truth.
I am already Love and Peace.
I let go of all the burdens of fear— I AM Love!

9

The Power of Peace

*"Peace I leave with you; my peace I give you.
I do not give to you as the world gives."*
John 14:27 NIV

Annie:

There have been times when I have not been at peace — peace seemed to have eluded me. Why? Was I trying too hard to capture it rather than being still and allowing peace to return? I now know that when I start relaxing into the Mind of the InVisible Presence something washes over me. I am again in that calm state of mind, in that place that only God and I reside.

Now I know that God is everywhere present. This means if I truly believe that the peace that passes all human understanding is from God, then I am also aware that peace surrounds me, enfolds me, and releases me from my wild imaginings.

Instead of being peace centered, I was "doing" centered. It is very clear that all I need to do, right now, is to stop thinking of what I can't or must do, and just think about God. My mind becomes still as I consider that "Peace, be still" pertains to me. I often tell others what peace means, but do I really know, deep within me, what peace is?

Deep within me is my clue. Deep within me, at the very core of my being, is a subtle knowing that all is well–no matter what I am experiencing in my mind, in my body, or in my affairs.

Years ago, I read something that Norman Vincent Peale said about being overwhelmed. He said to just call forth the most tranquil experience one has had and revisit it. At the time, I did not have any experience that I could classify as such.

However, sometime later, I realized that I just had such a memorable experience. It was aboard a cruise ship returning to Florida from the Caribbean. As I am an early riser —who has always enjoyed seeing the sun rise— I stole away to the top deck and was immediately engrossed in the most beautiful sky I have ever seen. The colors of amber, light blue, and shadows in dusky blues and grays made the sky appear as if I were beholding a lake surrounded by trees.

Now, whenever I desire, I can recall that sky in all its beauty and again become engrossed in it. Immediately, all my other thoughts are either washed away or engulfed in beauty.

Even now at this moment of writing, recalling this awesome experience, returns me to a state of peace — a serenity that passes me out of the doldrums into the beauty and awesome joy of life. Truly, this is the peace that passes all understanding.

How grateful I am to have the opportunity today to revisit peace.

I call forth the peace that is deep within my soul— *InVisible,* but fully present. And, at the same time, I also experience a wonderful calm moving throughout my body and mind.

I am totally content with my life as it is – busy, hectic, spontaneous, full with daily joys and periodic sorrow. No matter what the situation, I bask in peace. I am filled with the peace of God! Not as the world describes it, but only as God can provide.

Thank you, *Infinite Loving Presence*!

Bill:

Use your mind to create tranquility and Peace rather than allowing yourself to be upset from fears that do not exist.

Remind yourself you can choose peace anytime, anywhere. You control how you feel. You do not allow anyone to upset you.

When I think about the energy and feeling of being at Peace, I feel an inner calmness within myself. The peace of mind, body, and soul that we all can have.

Each one of us can start to find that inner peace by just taking a few moments to breathe and relax during the day. Finding the time in our busy schedules is important – just to let go and be ourselves.

Peace is the elimination of inner conflict. It is the ability to know you are loved in all things you do. It is the training of one's ego and putting aside the demands on us by others, so we can each connect and feel at peace.

Be open to change and allow yourself to live life fully with no regrets, no guilt, and no self-sabotaging thoughts about the past. Live fully in the present moment. Be happy, joyful, and connect to the source within.

10

The Power of Gratitude

"From everyone who has been given much, much will be demanded; and from the one who has been entrusted with much, much more will be asked."
Luke 12:48 NIV

Annie:

I recently attended an affair where everyone was gifted with a "gratitude" stone. We were asked to carry this stone with us or to place it where we would see it frequently to remind ourselves of the many "gifts" we continuously receive for which we could be grateful.

It matters not whether the gifts are large or small, courtesies that are extended to us by those familiar to us or from strangers—it only matters that the gifts are acknowledged with gratitude.

We were challenged to show our gratitude when others were the recipients of some good, to rejoice with them and for them.

As we chose our stones from the circulating basket, the presenter reminded us to not only be grateful for that which we receive, but also to rejoice when others received their good.

We experienced this feeling of loving gratitude when a woman who had the special "dot" on her program was entitled to receive the grand prize of the evening. When she raised her hand and received a lovely gift, everyone clapped. We were in a state of gratitude for her good and for each other's joy at seeing her joy as the recipient.

How thankful am I when someone other than me receives some measure of good during their day? Am I just grateful that I am not required to have chemo as others are, or am I also grateful that I have my health?

I have some friends who are retired and whose marriage of over 50 years continues. They travel extensively, and they entertain often. I am included in many of their activities, many times at their expense. Why? Because they are living a life filled with gratitude for the good they have, and they joyously share it.

Because I have fewer financial resources than this couple, I am not expected to reciprocate in the same manner. However, they constantly remind me that they appreciate my talents and what I bring to the mix.

I know that being content with what I have and the ability to share my talents wells up a sense of gratitude for just being alive.

Bill:

The first thing I do each morning before I get out of bed is to think of ten things for which I am grateful. By starting your day in a place of being grateful, you allow that positive energy to attract more things to you for which you can be grateful.

At first this new habit may only have a few things that come to mind. In a short time, you will find it easier to think of all the things for which you are grateful.

Allow yourself to expand and attract more of everything that is on your divine path. If you take the opposite position of never being grateful, pay attention to others around you who are not grateful and decide which type of life you want to live.

Being in harmony and radiating out a positive energy has always been more rewarding for me.

The more you pay attention to what you're grateful for, the less time you'll spend worrying about your fears, anxiety, work issues, relationship problems, or any other issues. These concerns will simply disappear like clouds drifting away.

I am grateful for the Love of God that is a part of me.
I am grateful I love and accept myself
as an expression of God.
I am grateful for the opportunities in my life.
I feel blessed I can meet the challenges of life
and find a solution.

There is an easy way to shift your awareness to seeing what is positive in your life. Start each day journaling about what you are grateful for. Within a few weeks you will be looking at your life through a different lens. Focus on how you feel when you see all the great things you have in your life. Then watch as the "snowball" of abundance keeps growing.

As an observer, I have seen many siblings that live in the same house growing up have a totally different view of life. One may only see what is wrong with their parents while the others are grateful to have parents who did the best that they knew how based on what they had learned from their own experiences in life.

For years I saw two sisters that had grown up in the same house and with the same parents. The older sister was happy with her life and lived with an expectation of wonder and knowing she would always have enough. However, the younger sister thought her parents should have taught them more about savings and financial budgeting and how to be more prepared for a financial crisis in life. Over time the younger sister could not forgive her parents for what they had not done. As she grew and raised her own family, she continued to struggle, seeming to never have anything extra to save. The older sister learned how to be grateful and kept attracting more good. Each of us have endless possibilities to be grateful.

We just need to practice remembering each day all for what we are grateful. Once you start that daily habit of reminding yourself of all that you are grateful for, you will also be able to believe more is possible.

Being grateful is not about boasting to others. Rather, it is also being able to be humble and generous, to inspire others by how you lead your life. It is having the ability to help our neighbors.

> *He is a wise man who does not grieve for the things which he has not but rejoices for those which he has. Epictetus*

11

The Power of Prayer

"Ask and it will be given to you; seek and you will find…"

Matthew 7:7 NIV

"This is the confidence we have in approaching God: that if we ask anything according to his will, he hears us.

1 John 5:14 NIV

Annie:

Prayer — asking, calling forth — is always occurring. Every time I say, "I want," I am praying for what I want to happen. Every time I say, "Have a good day," I am praying that you enjoy your activities to the fullest. Every time I call out in my mind or aloud through my words, I am praying.

However, I must remember that I am only calling forth that which God has already made available for I cannot call forth anything that God has not created.

Prayer then, for me, is calling forth God's power into my life or in the lives of others. In the prayer of Jabez (1 Chron:4), Jabez recognizes what he has and is now ready and for even a greater awareness of his good. The power in the prayer is recognizing God and knowing that all our needs are always met and met on time. I recognize that because God is all that I am, all that God has is already mine in accordance to my receptivity.

Because I have faith in God and believe that God is, and that it is God's good pleasure to give me what I sincerely desire, I trust that what I call forth manifests in my life at the time I call it forth.

I realize that when I align my desires with the desires or vision that God has for me (and for those for whom I pray), then the answer to my prayer is revealed in a myriad of ways.

Aligning my desires means that I ask only for what God desires in my prayer. I ask that God reveal to me that which I am to know, think, say, and do – as I become more willing to be an instrument through which some of the good of God flows.

I remember when my first grandchild was born. My daughter was experiencing complications and the baby "appeared" to be in danger of either not living or being severely affected because of lack of oxygen to his brain. I remember praying for hours that the child lives and be healthy and I finally released my prayer with "Your will be done," after which I fell into a deep sleep.

In the meantime, my son-in-law and his friends were rejoicing over his firstborn son. His was a prayer of thanksgiving— mine, a prayer of "misgivings" or misunderstanding of what God had called forth. Sometimes what we call prayer is only releasing our fears and forgetting that God is life—and in God there is no death.

In my misguided frustration and fears I agonized until at last I felt the release that with God all is well. (Note: my grandson is now a healthy husband and father).

Was my prayer powerful? Yes! It was answered in a way that I have clung to—that I am to bring my fears and frustrations, misgivings, and misunderstandings to God in prayer and my doubts of His power will be removed.

The power, then, is in my faith, my trust, and my belief that with God nothing (no thing) is impossible and that all things are within His Power.

My prayers are no longer an effort to "change" God or to change God's plan, but rather to become aligned with His perfect plan. The result: An *InVisible* Power moves through any and every experience which I face. Now, I pray for guidance, acceptance, joy, and peace for me as well as for all others involved. I endeavor to ask aright for that which I am praying.

I now more clearly understand what is meant by knowing the truth which makes one free. The *power of prayer* affords me the daily opportunity to know that there is a power and presence at the very essence of my being. It is the awesome, loving, and Infinite God within— ready to reveal to me the truth which makes me free to live an abundant and fulfilled life.

I now know that anything I pray for is already known and accomplished in the Mind of God. My power through prayer is to recognize this and to give all the glory to God. Sincere prayers by others opens our consciousness of this awesome communing with God on our behalf.

During a three-week period when my body was experiencing a debilitating illness, I was aware that more than 100 were praying for my physical as well as spiritual well-being. Even when I periodically doubted, I was uplifted by a call or a card simply stating: "You are in my prayers." This sharing of prayers kept me going until I fully agreed that where I was, the fullness of God was present and where God is, all is well.

What a gift we have been given—the awesome *InVisible Power of Prayer!*

Bill:

When I pray, I pray until I know the situation is complete and done. When starting my prayers, I always remember first that I am a part of God, the Holy Spirit—connected always with this universal truth of Love.

The more you pray, the more you will see changes happen in your life.

There are many things you can pray about. Remember to acknowledge your relationship with being in Spirit, being connected to all, being in peace, love, and joy.

Praying is easy. It is a simple conversation with you and the Holy Spirit within you. It is connecting to the Divine Spirit, Energy, and focusing on the feeling you have when asking for what is already so. See and feel your request for yourself or another person in the present moment.

There are many ways to pray. Many finds being seated or standing in one place works well. A minister once told me he prays while doing his morning walk. He said this is best if you are walking alone or not encountering anyone you who would want to stop and talk with you.

I can picture him on these walks as he repeated his prayers. What a great way to start your day—being one with God and getting some exercise done.

When you pray, pray for it all. Pray big prayers. If you are in a physically abusive relationship, don't just pray for the courage to endure the pain, rather pray for the courage to move on and to be open to a loving, fulfilling relationship.

Pray also for others' highest and best good, but not to change them.

If you have a boss which you feel is terrible, don't just pray for patience to put up with your boss, rather pray big for the opportunity to be free to accomplish more and enjoy the job you do—for the highest good of all.

If a family member has a drug addiction problem, don't pray "I hope they won't steal anything from me to support buying drugs." Rather, pray that they sense and feel that they are surrounded with the love of God and family, that they will know they have choices and that they can turn their life around and be happy and fulfilled without using drugs.

If a co-worker is stressed over working with those who do not seem to take their participation seriously and cannot count on their team to accomplish the tasks, don't ask for new "clowns." Rather, ask that your co-workers will be able to see a plan to help the situation and accomplish their goals by the deadlines given. Pray that all the co-workers will be able to work together in harmony.

12

The Power of Stillness

"...Be still and know that I am God..."
Psalm 46:10 NIV

Annie:

Something incredible happens to me when I still myself– that is, when I let go of all outer distractions and become receptive to listening and communing with the *indwelling power and presence within me*. It is not always easy to do this– for the "story" on the television, or the ache in my knee, or the hunger pang attracts my attention.

But as I repeat in a whisper to my mind "Be still and know that I AM" something returns or transports me to that place of quiet – that place of serenity – that place of knowing that all is well, right now.

It is in this quietness that I am bathed in a knowingness that where I am, the fullness of God is. I can again regain my understanding that the great I AM within me is working out whatever issue I thought I had.

A plaque on the front wall of our Sanctuary reads: "Be Still and Know that I AM …" The gentleman who suggested the three dots at the end of this quote said that God was and is always what we need at any moment when we call forth the experience we desire. Therefore, the dots are to be replaced with the words we each desire at that time

For instance, when I feel weak, I can say "Be still and know that I AM your strength and vitality." Or, if I am depressed I can say "Be still and know that I AM your joy." When I feel ill, I can say "Be still and know that I AM your health."

Entering the Stillness also allows me to release any thoughts of inadequacy, impotency, hate, or judgement I may be harboring in my heart. When I am still and am only thinking of God, I find that I cannot hate or judge or feel inadequate. I also use this awareness to speak my words for others who ask for prayers. I become still and again realize that where the person is, the fullness of God is. My statement might be "Be still and know that I AM where Jane is," or I just know without a doubt that where that person is, God is, and where God is, Good is, and where Good is, divine right action always is.

In the stillness I remember who I am and who God is—inseparable—and that no person, condition, or thing has any power in my life, that only God has power in my life and in all of life for there is no other outside of God. In my stillness I remember that God is ALL there is, and that God is that which lives in me, that which breaths through me, and that which is expressed as me. And, because God is Omnipresent, I remember that God is living in, through, from, and as all simultaneously.

Bill:

In the quiet moment of being still, calming the mind, feeling the stillness and oneness of God that is where you are – connect consciously to and in Spirit. There are no words that can express the all-encompassing energy that is part of you always. I imagine each of us has this ability since we are all created in the likeness of God. I am aware that each person may have their own unique experiences.

Stillness can be achieved by meditation, breathing techniques, or by focusing all your attention on the moment while you pray.

An easy way to accomplish getting to a place of feeling this stillness is by breathing. Count the number of breaths you take in two minutes. Then, wherever you are (when *not* operating machinery like driving, etc.), just close your eyes, focus on counting your breaths until you reach the same number. This will give you a quick two-minute example of how to calm and be still in the moment.

Choose peace, love and joy for yourself and all others. You are always a part of God. Remember to take time each day to re-connect consciously and be in the Spirit.

An Inward Stillness
Henry Wadsworth Longfellow

Let us labor then for an inward stillness,
An inward stillness and an inward healing
That perfect silence where the lips and heart
Are still, and we no longer entertain
Our own imperfect thoughts and vain opinions,

But God alone speaks in us, and we wait
In singleness of heart, that we may know
His will and, in the silence of our spirits,
That we may do His will and do that only.

Epilogue

Our InVisible World became increasingly visible to us as we sought the Indwelling Infinite Presence to reveal Its truth, Its beauty and Its love to both of us. We experienced a new appreciation for all of life, whether our own or another's.

During this process, we found a new and joyous outlook— for we know that there is much, much more to life than we see with our eyes or hear with our ears. We know that it is unconditioned love!

> *"Eye has not seen, nor ear heard, nor have entered into the heart of man, the things which God has prepared for those who love Him."*
>
> *1 Corinthians, 2:9 KJV*

> *"The LORD is good to those whose hope is in him, to the one who seeks him."*
>
> *Lamentations 3:25 NIV*

Bill Anderson

Mr. Bill Anderson has had a successful career managing large software development projects for several Fortune 100 companies. His background is in engineering, accounting, and information services.

Early in life his desire to learn more than what church or school could teach him about spiritual truth led him on a path of self-discovery. Now, he shares his knowledge: how to truly realize each person's potential. He also aspires to let everyone know how simple it is to utilize the power within to be our own source of happiness, love, and connection to all living things.

Bill resides in St. Louis, Missouri.

Annie P. Clark

Annie P. Clark is an ordained minister. She founded *Radiance Center for Spiritual Living*, retiring after serving as its spiritual leader for 21 years. She is a graduate of Holmes Institute (formerly Ernest Holmes College, School of Ministry) and later served on its faculty in St. Louis, Missouri.

Her current ministry, *Inner Splendor*, serves people of all faiths through *"Spiritual Explorations"*—a gathering of individuals seeking to explore, examine, and uncover their personal beliefs and understanding of life issues. She conducts metaphysical Bible studies, facilitates spiritual retreats and workshops, and is a frequent guest speaker at area churches and civic events.

Annie is a member in the Metro-East Interfaith Partnership and is a board member of the Eagle's Nest of St. Clair County, serving homeless veterans.

She resides in Shiloh, Illinois.